PRINCEWILL LAGANG

The Social Media Entrepreneur: Building Brands Online

First published by PRINCEWILL LAGANG 2023

Copyright © 2023 by Princewill Lagang

All rights reserved. No part of this publication may be reproduced, stored or transmitted in any form or by any means, electronic, mechanical, photocopying, recording, scanning, or otherwise without written permission from the publisher. It is illegal to copy this book, post it to a website, or distribute it by any other means without permission.

Princewill Lagang asserts the moral right to be identified as the author of this work.

First edition

This book was professionally typeset on Reedsy.
Find out more at reedsy.com

Contents

1. The Social Media Landscape — 1
2. Defining Your Niche — 4
3. Crafting Compelling Content — 7
4. Growing Your Audience — 11
5. Monetizing Your Online Presence — 15
6. Building a Strong Brand Identity — 19
7. Scaling Your Brand and Business — 23
8. Staying Relevant in the Digital Landscape — 26
9. Managing Challenges and Navigating Pitfalls — 30
10. Your Path to Ongoing Success — 34
11. Conclusion and Looking Ahead — 38
12. Additional Resources and Next Steps — 41
13. Summary — 45

1

The Social Media Landscape

In today's digital age, the internet has transformed the way we live, work, and interact. Social media, in particular, has emerged as a powerful tool that can change the trajectory of businesses and personal brands. In this chapter, we will embark on a journey to explore the dynamic world of social media entrepreneurship and discover the strategies and principles that will help you build successful brands online.

The Rise of Social Media

The digital revolution has brought about significant changes in the way we communicate and connect. Social media platforms like Facebook, Twitter, Instagram, and LinkedIn have become integral parts of our lives, providing us with unprecedented access to a global audience. But what sets social media apart is its potential for entrepreneurship and brand building.

We've witnessed the rise of social media influencers, individuals who have leveraged these platforms to build personal brands and generate income. Their success stories are often remarkable, from beauty bloggers who have launched their cosmetics lines to fitness enthusiasts who have transformed their passion into lucrative careers. These individuals have capitalized on the power of social media, and their stories serve as an inspiration to aspiring social media entrepreneurs.

The Entrepreneurial Spirit

Entrepreneurship has always been a driving force behind innovation and progress. It's about identifying opportunities, taking calculated risks, and creating value. In the digital age, these opportunities have extended to the online realm. Entrepreneurs are no longer limited to brick-and-mortar businesses; they are now building digital empires through the internet's vast potential.

Social media entrepreneurs are individuals who embody this entrepreneurial spirit, using social platforms as their canvas to craft new narratives, products, and services. They understand that social media offers a unique set of tools and tactics to reach, engage, and influence audiences, enabling them to create thriving brands.

Navigating the Digital Landscape

The digital landscape is vast and constantly evolving. To succeed as a social media entrepreneur, it's crucial to understand the intricacies of various social platforms, algorithms, and user behavior. In this book, we will explore the nuances of popular platforms, delve into the psychology of social media, and discuss strategies for effective brand building.

Whether you're a seasoned entrepreneur looking to expand your online presence or someone entirely new to the world of social media, this book will provide you with the insights and knowledge needed to embark on a successful journey as a social media entrepreneur.

What's Ahead

In the following chapters, we will dive deep into the core principles of social media entrepreneurship. We'll explore how to define your niche, build a personal brand, create compelling content, grow your audience, and monetize your online presence. The journey will be filled with challenges and opportunities, but with the right mindset and strategies, you can make your mark in the world of social media entrepreneurship.

Are you ready to embark on this exciting journey? Let's begin by understanding the social media landscape and the vast opportunities it offers for entrepreneurs and brand builders alike. In the chapters to come, we'll equip you with the knowledge and skills you need to thrive in the digital age.

2

Defining Your Niche

In Chapter 1, we explored the landscape of social media entrepreneurship and its immense potential. Now, in Chapter 2, we will delve into one of the fundamental aspects of building a successful online brand: defining your niche. Your niche is the unique corner of the market that you'll focus on, and it's crucial to your success as a social media entrepreneur.

The Power of a Niche

In a vast sea of digital content, finding your niche is like discovering your own island. It's your unique space where you can plant your flag and stand out. Your niche defines what you're passionate about, what you're knowledgeable in, and what sets you apart from the competition.

Choosing a niche allows you to target a specific audience, creating content that resonates with them, and establishing your authority and credibility within that area. It's essential for creating a strong and loyal online community.

Identifying Your Passion and Expertise

DEFINING YOUR NICHE

The first step in defining your niche is to identify your passion and expertise. What are you genuinely interested in? What are you knowledgeable about? What topics or activities make you excited to create content on a regular basis?

Your passion and expertise will be the driving force behind your online presence. If you're genuinely passionate about your niche, it will come across in your content and interactions, making it more relatable and authentic.

Researching and Validating Your Niche

Once you've identified your passion and expertise, it's important to research and validate your niche. Is there an audience for what you want to share? Are there other influencers or brands successfully operating in this space?

Market research and competitive analysis are essential to determine if your chosen niche is viable. You'll want to look for opportunities, gaps in content, and areas where you can differentiate yourself.

Narrowing Down Your Focus

Sometimes, a niche may be broad, and it can be beneficial to narrow down your focus. For example, if you're passionate about travel, you might choose to specialize in budget travel, adventure travel, or luxury travel. Narrowing down your focus can help you target a specific audience and establish yourself as an expert in a particular sub-niche.

The Importance of Authenticity

Authenticity is a cornerstone of successful social media entrepreneurship. Be true to yourself and your niche. Don't choose a niche solely for its potential popularity or profitability if it doesn't align with your values and interests. Authenticity will help you build trust with your audience, which is essential for long-term success.

What's Ahead

In the next chapters, we'll explore the practical steps for building your online brand within your chosen niche. This includes creating content, growing your audience, and developing a brand strategy that aligns with your niche. Defining your niche is just the first step on your journey as a social media entrepreneur, but it's a crucial one.

Now that you've identified your niche, it's time to dive into creating content that resonates with your audience. Chapter 3 will guide you through the process of crafting compelling and engaging content that sets you on the path to online success.

3

Crafting Compelling Content

Content is the heart and soul of your online presence. In Chapter 2, we discussed the importance of defining your niche, and now it's time to explore how to create content that resonates with your audience. This chapter will guide you through the process of crafting compelling and engaging content that sets you on the path to online success.

The Art of Content Creation

Content is what draws your audience in, keeps them engaged, and makes them want to come back for more. It can take various forms, including written articles, videos, images, infographics, podcasts, and more. To be a successful social media entrepreneur, you need to master the art of content creation.

Understanding Your Audience

Before you start creating content, it's essential to understand your target audience. Who are they? What are their interests, problems, and preferences? What kind of content are they looking for?

Understanding your audience is crucial for tailoring your content to meet their needs and expectations. This requires research and ongoing engagement with your followers to stay attuned to their feedback and interests.

Planning Your Content Strategy

A well-thought-out content strategy is the backbone of your online presence. It includes a content calendar, themes, and a plan for consistent posting. Your strategy should reflect the following:

1. Content Types: Determine the types of content that work best for your niche and audience. This may include written blog posts, video tutorials, Instagram stories, or a combination of various formats.

2. Frequency: Decide how often you'll post content. Consistency is key, so set a realistic schedule that you can maintain.

3. Themes: Develop themes or topics that align with your niche and appeal to your audience's interests.

4. Keywords: Incorporate relevant keywords that can help your content get discovered through search engines and social media platforms.

Creating Engaging Content

Engaging content is content that captures your audience's attention and encourages interaction. Here are some tips for creating engaging content:

1. Storytelling: Weave stories into your content to make it relatable and memorable.

2. Visual Appeal: Use high-quality images, videos, and graphics to make your content visually appealing.

3. Value: Provide value to your audience through informative, entertaining, or educational content.

4. Interactivity: Encourage comments, likes, shares, and other forms of engagement by asking questions and involving your audience.

5. Consistency: Maintain a consistent style and tone to establish your brand identity.

Leveraging Various Platforms

Different social media platforms have their unique content requirements. For example, Instagram is highly visual, while Twitter emphasizes concise, text-based content. Tailor your content to suit the platform you're using, making the most of its features and audience expectations.

Monitoring and Iterating

Regularly monitor the performance of your content. Pay attention to engagement metrics like likes, comments, shares, and views. Use analytics tools to understand what's working and what isn't. Then, iterate and refine your content strategy based on the data you collect.

What's Ahead

Chapter 3 has provided you with the essential building blocks of content creation. In the upcoming chapters, we will explore strategies for growing your audience, monetizing your online presence, and developing a brand identity that aligns with your niche.

As you continue your journey as a social media entrepreneur, remember that content creation is an ongoing process that requires dedication and creativity. Your ability to craft compelling content will be a key driver of your success in the digital world.

4

Growing Your Audience

In the previous chapters, we discussed the importance of defining your niche and creating compelling content. Now, in Chapter 4, we'll explore the crucial aspect of growing your audience. Building a dedicated and engaged following is essential for the success of your social media entrepreneurship journey.

The Significance of a Strong Audience

Your audience is the community that supports and interacts with your content. A strong and engaged audience can help you in various ways:

- Visibility: A larger audience means more people see your content, expanding your reach and potential influence.

- Credibility: A substantial and engaged following adds to your credibility and authority within your niche.

- Monetization Opportunities: A bigger audience opens doors to various monetization options, such as sponsored posts, affiliate marketing, and selling your products or services.

- Feedback and Insights: Engaged followers can provide valuable feedback and insights, helping you refine your content and strategies.

Strategies for Audience Growth

Growing your audience takes time and effort, but with the right strategies, you can steadily increase your follower count. Here are some key tactics:

1. Consistency

Consistency in posting is essential. Your audience should know when to expect new content from you. Create a content calendar and stick to it.

2. Engagement

Engage with your audience by responding to comments, starting conversations, and showing appreciation for their support. Engagement fosters a sense of community.

3. Collaborations

Collaborate with other influencers or brands in your niche. Cross-promotion can introduce you to new audiences and boost your credibility.

4. Hashtags

Use relevant and trending hashtags to increase the discoverability of your content. Research and select the best hashtags for each post.

5. Contest and Giveaways

Organize contests or giveaways to encourage user participation and attract new followers. These can create excitement and engagement.

6. Content Optimization

Optimize your content for search engines and social media algorithms. Use keywords and descriptions that align with your niche and attract your target audience.

7. Guest Posting

Consider guest posting on other platforms or blogs related to your niche. This can expose you to a new audience and establish your authority.

8. Paid Advertising

Invest in paid social media advertising to reach a broader audience. Platforms like Facebook and Instagram offer targeted advertising options.

Audience Quality vs. Quantity

While it's essential to grow your audience, quality matters more than quantity. An engaged and genuinely interested audience is far more valuable than a large but uninterested one. Focus on building relationships with your followers and providing value.

Monitoring and Adjusting

Keep a close eye on your audience's growth and engagement metrics. Analyze what's working and what's not, and adjust your strategies accordingly. Remember that growth is often gradual, so stay patient and persistent.

What's Ahead

As your audience grows, so do the opportunities for monetizing your online presence. In Chapter 5, we will explore various methods of monetization, including sponsored content, affiliate marketing, and selling your products or services. Growing your audience is just one step on your journey to becoming a successful social media entrepreneur, and it paves the way for the next exciting chapters of your adventure.

5

Monetizing Your Online Presence

In the previous chapters, we explored the essentials of social media entrepreneurship, including defining your niche, crafting compelling content, and growing your audience. Now, in Chapter 5, we'll dive into the exciting world of monetizing your online presence. Turning your passion and hard work into a source of income is a significant milestone in your journey.

The Diversity of Monetization Methods

Monetization means converting your online presence into revenue. There are various ways to do this, and your choice of methods should align with your niche, audience, and personal goals. Here are some common monetization methods:

1. Sponsored Content

Companies may pay you to create content that features their products or services. Sponsored posts should align with your niche and be disclosed to your audience transparently.

2. Affiliate Marketing

You can earn a commission by promoting other people's or companies' products or services through unique affiliate links. Whenever a purchase is made through your link, you receive a percentage of the sale.

3. Selling Products or Services

Create and sell your products or services related to your niche. This could include eBooks, online courses, merchandise, or personalized services such as coaching or consulting.

4. Ad Revenue

If your online presence generates a substantial amount of traffic, you can earn revenue through ad placements on your website, blog, or YouTube channel. Platforms like Google AdSense can help with this.

5. Crowdfunding

Some content creators rely on platforms like Patreon, Kickstarter, or GoFundMe, where their dedicated followers support them financially in exchange for exclusive content or rewards.

6. Membership Subscriptions

Offer exclusive content to paying subscribers. Platforms like Patreon and Substack are popular choices for this model.

7. Consulting and Speaking Engagements

Leverage your expertise in your niche to offer consulting services or speak at conferences and events for a fee.

8. Product Reviews and Endorsements

Apart from sponsored content, you can review and endorse products or services you genuinely believe in. Brands may compensate you for your expertise and endorsement.

Choosing the Right Monetization Mix

The most successful social media entrepreneurs often use a combination of these monetization methods. Diversifying your income streams reduces risk and can lead to more stable and substantial revenue over time.

When choosing your monetization mix, consider your niche, audience preferences, and your own strengths and interests. You may also need to adapt and experiment with different methods to find what works best for you.

Ethical Considerations

Monetization should be done with ethics and transparency in mind. Always disclose sponsored content and affiliate links, be honest in product reviews, and prioritize your audience's trust and satisfaction. Overpromoting or selling low-quality products can damage your brand and reputation.

Planning and Financial Management

With monetization comes financial responsibility. It's essential to plan your income, manage your expenses, and consider taxes and legal obligations. Set financial goals and consider investing in your brand, such as upgrading equipment or attending relevant courses or conferences.

What's Ahead

As your online presence continues to grow and generate revenue, it's time to consider brand development and strategy. In Chapter 6, we'll explore how to establish a strong and consistent brand identity that aligns with your niche and attracts your target audience. Monetization is a significant milestone in your journey, and brand development will help ensure long-term success as a social media entrepreneur.

6

Building a Strong Brand Identity

In the previous chapters, we've discussed defining your niche, creating compelling content, growing your audience, and monetizing your online presence. Now, in Chapter 6, we'll explore the critical aspect of building a strong brand identity. Your brand is the essence of who you are and what you represent in the digital world.

The Significance of Brand Identity

Your brand identity is more than just a logo and color scheme. It encompasses your values, mission, voice, and the unique personality you bring to your online presence. A strong brand identity:

- Builds Trust: Consistency in your brand identity creates trust with your audience. They know what to expect from you.

- Differentiates You: In a crowded digital space, your brand sets you apart. It's what makes you memorable.

- Fosters Loyalty: A strong brand identity can lead to loyal followers who engage with your content and support your endeavors.

Elements of Brand Identity

To create a strong brand identity, you'll need to consider several key elements:

1. Brand Name and Tagline

Choose a name that is memorable and relevant to your niche. A tagline can succinctly convey your mission or unique selling proposition.

2. Logo and Visuals

Create a visually appealing logo and establish a consistent color palette, typography, and imagery. These visual elements should reflect your brand's personality.

3. Tone and Voice

Define your brand's tone and voice. Are you humorous, authoritative, or friendly? Your tone should align with your niche and resonate with your target audience.

4. Values and Mission

Identify your brand's core values and mission. What do you stand for, and what do you hope to achieve with your online presence?

5. Content Style

Your content should reflect your brand identity. Whether it's blog posts, videos, or social media updates, maintain a consistent style that is recognizable as yours.

6. Audience Engagement

How you engage with your audience also contributes to your brand identity. Are you responsive, supportive, or informative? Your interactions should reflect your brand's values.

Consistency Is Key

Consistency is the cornerstone of a strong brand identity. Ensure that all elements of your brand are aligned and cohesive. Your audience should instantly recognize your content, even when it appears in different places or formats.

Evolving Your Brand

As your online presence grows and evolves, your brand identity may also change. It's important to periodically evaluate and adjust your brand to reflect your personal growth, changes in your niche, and shifts in your audience's preferences.

Authenticity

A genuine and authentic brand identity is essential. Don't try to be someone you're not or create a brand that doesn't align with your true self. Authenticity resonates with audiences and builds trust.

What's Ahead

With a strong and consistent brand identity in place, you'll have a solid foundation for long-term success as a social media entrepreneur. In the next chapters, we'll explore advanced strategies for scaling your brand, managing your online presence, and staying relevant in an ever-evolving digital landscape. Building your brand identity is a significant step in your journey, and it sets the stage for the exciting chapters ahead.

7

Scaling Your Brand and Business

In the previous chapters, we discussed defining your niche, creating compelling content, growing your audience, monetizing your online presence, and building a strong brand identity. Now, in Chapter 7, we'll explore the strategies for scaling your brand and business to achieve even greater success as a social media entrepreneur.

The Power of Scaling

Scaling your brand and business means taking it to the next level. It involves expanding your reach, growing your revenue, and increasing your impact. Here are some reasons why scaling is essential:

- Reaching More People: Scaling allows you to reach a broader audience and impact more lives with your content and products.

- Diversifying Income Streams: Expanding your brand can lead to additional income streams and reduce your reliance on a single source of revenue.

- Building Authority: As your brand grows, you'll naturally build authority and influence in your niche.

- Creating Long-Term Sustainability: Scaling can help ensure that your online presence remains sustainable and relevant over time.

Strategies for Scaling

1. Diversification

Consider diversifying your content and monetization methods. For instance, if you've primarily focused on written content, start incorporating video or podcasts. Explore additional revenue streams like online courses, consulting, or public speaking engagements.

2. Partnerships and Collaborations

Collaborate with other influencers, brands, or experts in your niche. Joint ventures can introduce you to new audiences and amplify your brand.

3. Product Development

Invest in the development of new products or services that align with your niche and audience's needs. This could be expanding your merchandise line, creating premium content, or launching a subscription model.

4. Automation and Delegation

As your brand grows, you may need to automate certain tasks or delegate them to a team. This can free up your time to focus on creating high-impact content and strategies.

5. Data Analysis

Use data analytics to understand your audience better and fine-tune your strategies. Data can provide insights into what's working and what needs improvement.

6. Personal Growth

Continuously invest in your personal and professional growth. As the face of your brand, your development can have a significant impact on your brand's success.

Staying True to Your Core Values

While scaling your brand is essential for growth, it's equally important to stay true to your core values and brand identity. Make sure that your expansion aligns with your mission and that you maintain the authenticity and integrity that made your brand successful in the first place.

Avoiding Burnout

Scaling can be challenging and time-consuming. To avoid burnout, set boundaries, manage your time effectively, and consider seeking support from professionals, mentors, or coaches.

What's Ahead

Scaling your brand and business is an exciting and challenging phase in your journey as a social media entrepreneur. In the upcoming chapters, we'll explore advanced strategies for managing your online presence, handling challenges, and staying relevant in an ever-evolving digital landscape. Scaling your brand represents a significant leap forward, and it opens up new possibilities for your online venture.

8

Staying Relevant in the Digital Landscape

In the previous chapters, we explored the essentials of building a brand online, from defining your niche and creating compelling content to monetizing your presence and scaling your business. Now, in Chapter 8, we'll delve into the strategies for staying relevant and maintaining your success in the ever-evolving digital landscape.

The Dynamic Nature of the Digital World

The digital world is constantly changing. New platforms emerge, algorithms evolve, and audience preferences shift. To stay relevant as a social media entrepreneur, it's crucial to adapt to these changes and embrace the dynamism of the online sphere.

Continuous Learning and Adaptation

Remaining relevant requires a commitment to continuous learning and adaptation. Here are some strategies to help you stay ahead in the digital landscape:

STAYING RELEVANT IN THE DIGITAL LANDSCAPE

1. Stay Informed

Keep a close eye on industry trends, technological advancements, and changes in social media platforms. Subscribe to relevant newsletters, follow thought leaders, and attend webinars or conferences.

2. Experiment and Innovate

Don't be afraid to experiment with new content formats, platforms, or monetization methods. Innovation often leads to fresh opportunities for growth and engagement.

3. Audience Feedback

Regularly seek feedback from your audience. Use polls, surveys, and direct interactions to understand their changing needs and preferences.

4. Collaborate

Collaborations with other influencers or experts in your niche can introduce you to new ideas and strategies. They can also help you reach broader audiences.

5. Content Quality

Maintain a high standard for your content. Quality content resonates with your audience, fosters engagement, and keeps them coming back for more.

6. Consistency

While adapting is crucial, consistency in your brand identity and content schedule is equally important. Balance innovation with the core elements that define your brand.

7. Content Optimization

Optimize your content for search engines and social media algorithms. Learn how to leverage these tools to ensure your content reaches its intended audience.

Building Resilience

Staying relevant often requires resilience. You may face challenges, criticism, or changes in your niche's landscape. Here are some tips for building resilience:

- Develop a Growth Mindset: Embrace challenges as opportunities for growth and learning. A growth mindset allows you to adapt more effectively.

- Mental and Emotional Health: Take care of your mental and emotional well-being. This includes managing stress, seeking support when needed, and maintaining a work-life balance.

- Stay True to Your Values: While adapting is important, ensure that you stay aligned with your core values and brand identity.

Preparing for the Future

The digital landscape will continue to evolve, and being prepared for the future is essential. Consider the following:

- Emerging Technologies: Keep an eye on emerging technologies like augmented reality, virtual reality, and artificial intelligence, as they may impact the way content is created and consumed.

- Diversify Your Digital Footprint: Explore other platforms and online ventures to spread your digital presence. This can mitigate risks associated with changes on a single platform.

- Networking and Support: Build a network of peers, mentors, and professionals who can offer guidance and support as you navigate the evolving digital landscape.

What's Ahead

Staying relevant in the digital landscape is an ongoing process that requires adaptability and a commitment to learning and innovation. In the upcoming chapters, we'll explore advanced strategies for managing your online presence, handling challenges, and achieving long-term success as a social media entrepreneur. Adapting to the dynamic digital world is a key factor in ensuring your brand's continued relevance and success.

9

Managing Challenges and Navigating Pitfalls

In the previous chapters, we've explored the journey of building a brand online, from defining your niche and creating compelling content to monetizing your presence, scaling your business, and staying relevant in the digital landscape. Now, in Chapter 9, we'll tackle the inevitable challenges and pitfalls that social media entrepreneurs encounter and how to navigate them successfully.

The Reality of Challenges

While the world of social media entrepreneurship is filled with opportunities and rewards, it's not without its challenges. Understanding and proactively managing these challenges is crucial for sustaining and growing your online brand.

Common Challenges and Strategies

Let's delve into some of the most common challenges faced by social media entrepreneurs and how to address them:

1. Burnout

Challenge: The fast-paced, demanding nature of social media can lead to burnout, impacting your creativity and productivity.

Strategy: Implement a structured work schedule, take regular breaks, and prioritize self-care. Delegate tasks when necessary and maintain a work-life balance to prevent burnout.

2. Algorithm Changes

Challenge: Social media algorithms can change, affecting the reach and engagement of your content.

Strategy: Stay informed about algorithm updates, adapt your content strategy accordingly, and diversify your digital presence to reduce reliance on a single platform.

3. Negative Feedback

Challenge: Negative comments or criticism can be disheartening and challenging to handle.

Strategy: Develop a thick skin and focus on constructive criticism. Use negative feedback as an opportunity to improve and engage in a respectful manner.

4. Fierce Competition

Challenge: The digital landscape is highly competitive, with many entrepreneurs vying for attention in your niche.

Strategy: Differentiate yourself through your brand identity, innovative content, and genuine engagement with your audience. Collaboration and networking can also help you stand out.

5. Legal and Ethical Issues

Challenge: Navigating legal matters, such as copyright issues or disclosure requirements for sponsored content, can be complex.

Strategy: Educate yourself about legal regulations in your niche and seek legal advice when necessary. Always act ethically and transparently to maintain trust.

6. Staying Fresh and Innovative

Challenge: Sustaining innovation in your content can be challenging over time.

Strategy: Embrace continuous learning, seek inspiration from diverse sources, and explore new content formats to keep your audience engaged.

7. Handling Growth

Challenge: Rapid growth can be overwhelming, leading to organizational and scalability issues.

Strategy: Plan for growth by automating tasks, delegating responsibilities, and establishing efficient workflows. Invest in tools and systems that support your expansion.

8. Adapting to New Technologies

Challenge: Adapting to emerging technologies can be daunting for those not technologically inclined.

Strategy: Invest in education and training to stay updated on new technologies relevant to your niche. Consider collaborating with experts if needed.

Cultivating Resilience

Resilience is key to overcoming challenges. Develop a mindset that embraces setbacks as opportunities for growth. Seek support from peers, mentors, and professionals to help navigate difficult situations.

Preparing for the Future

As the digital landscape continues to evolve, staying proactive and adaptable is essential. Embrace change as an opportunity for improvement, and always remain aligned with your brand's core values and mission.

What's Ahead

As you face and conquer challenges in your journey as a social media entrepreneur, you'll continue to learn and grow. In the final chapter of this book, we'll summarize the key takeaways and offer a roadmap for your ongoing success in building and maintaining a thriving online brand. Managing challenges is an integral part of your entrepreneurial journey, and the skills you develop will strengthen your brand over time.

10

Your Path to Ongoing Success

Congratulations! You've journeyed through the intricacies of social media entrepreneurship, from defining your niche and creating compelling content to growing your audience, monetizing your online presence, building a strong brand identity, staying relevant, and managing the challenges that come your way. In this final chapter, we'll summarize the key takeaways and offer a roadmap for your ongoing success in building and maintaining a thriving online brand.

Key Takeaways

Throughout this book, we've covered a range of topics and strategies for your journey as a social media entrepreneur. Let's recap some of the essential lessons:

1. Defining Your Niche: Your niche is the foundation of your brand. It's crucial to choose a niche you're passionate about and that aligns with your expertise and values.

2. Creating Compelling Content: Quality content is the lifeblood of your

brand. Ensure it's engaging, valuable, and resonates with your audience.

3. Growing Your Audience: Building a dedicated and engaged following is essential for success. Consistency, engagement, and collaboration are key strategies for audience growth.

4. Monetizing Your Presence: Multiple monetization methods are available, from sponsored content and affiliate marketing to selling your products or services. Diversify your income streams.

5. Building a Strong Brand Identity: Your brand identity includes your name, logo, values, and the unique personality you bring to your online presence. Consistency is vital.

6. Staying Relevant: The digital landscape is dynamic. Continuous learning, adaptation, and innovation are essential for staying relevant in the online world.

7. Managing Challenges: Challenges are a part of the journey. Strategies for handling burnout, algorithm changes, negative feedback, competition, legal issues, and growth are crucial for your resilience.

Your Roadmap to Ongoing Success

Now, let's outline a roadmap for your ongoing success as a social media entrepreneur:

1. Continuous Learning

Commit to lifelong learning. Stay informed about industry trends, technological advancements, and emerging platforms. Attend webinars, read industry publications, and engage with thought leaders to remain at the forefront of your niche.

2. Content Innovation

Continuously innovate with your content. Experiment with new formats and platforms to keep your audience engaged. Seek inspiration from diverse sources to infuse freshness into your work.

3. Consistent Brand Identity

Maintain the integrity of your brand identity. It's your signature in the digital landscape. Ensure that all elements, from your name and logo to your values and tone, remain consistent across platforms.

4. Adapt to Change

Embrace change as an opportunity for growth. Be proactive in adapting to evolving algorithms, audience preferences, and technological advancements. Diversify your digital footprint to mitigate risks.

5. Resilience and Support

Cultivate resilience in the face of challenges. Seek support from mentors, peers, and professionals. Develop a growth mindset that views setbacks as opportunities for improvement.

6. Reflect and Refine

Regularly assess your brand's performance. Analyze audience metrics and feedback. Reflect on your journey and refine your strategies to align with your goals and evolving audience needs.

Your Ongoing Success

The journey of a social media entrepreneur is dynamic and filled with opportunities for growth and impact. With continuous learning, adaptation, and a commitment to authenticity and quality, you're well-equipped for ongoing success in the digital landscape.

11

Conclusion and Looking Ahead

In the preceding chapters, we've embarked on a comprehensive exploration of the world of social media entrepreneurship. We've delved into the essential elements that contribute to your success, from defining your niche and crafting compelling content to growing your audience, monetizing your online presence, building a strong brand identity, staying relevant, and managing the challenges that come your way. As we conclude this journey, let's reflect on the path you've taken and look ahead to the exciting possibilities that await.

Celebrating Your Achievements

First and foremost, take a moment to celebrate your achievements. The journey of a social media entrepreneur is not without its challenges, and your commitment and passion have brought you to this point. You've built a brand that resonates with your audience, and you've harnessed the power of the digital world to make a positive impact.

The Ongoing Adventure

CONCLUSION AND LOOKING AHEAD

Your journey doesn't end here; it's an ongoing adventure. The digital landscape will continue to evolve, and your brand will grow, adapt, and inspire. Here are some key takeaways and ideas for the road ahead:

Embrace Change

The digital world is dynamic. Be open to change, and view it as an opportunity for growth. Stay informed about emerging trends, platforms, and technologies, and be willing to innovate and adapt to remain relevant.

Leverage Your Brand Identity

Your brand identity is your compass. Stay consistent with your core values, mission, and unique personality. It's your authenticity and relatability that make your brand stand out in the crowded online space.

Cultivate Resilience

Challenges are part of the journey. Develop the resilience to overcome setbacks and the wisdom to learn from them. Seek support from mentors, peers, and professionals to navigate difficult situations.

Prioritize Quality

Quality content is your most potent tool. Continue to invest in creating valuable, engaging content that resonates with your audience. Innovate with new formats and stay true to your style.

Evolve and Diversify

As your brand grows, consider diversifying your presence. Explore new content formats, platforms, or monetization methods to expand your reach and mitigate risks associated with relying on a single source of revenue.

Give Back

Your success allows you to give back to your community and causes that matter to you. Use your platform to make a positive impact, whether through charitable initiatives, awareness campaigns, or supporting meaningful causes.

Your Ongoing Success

The journey of a social media entrepreneur is a dynamic and fulfilling one. It's filled with opportunities to inspire, connect, and create. Your brand has the potential to make a meaningful difference in the lives of your audience and the digital communities you're part of.

As you move forward, continue to learn, adapt, and create with passion and authenticity. The world of social media entrepreneurship is an ever-evolving one, and your dedication will shape the future of your brand and the impact you make in the digital landscape.

12

Additional Resources and Next Steps

Congratulations on completing this comprehensive journey through the world of social media entrepreneurship! You've gained a wealth of knowledge and insights to guide your brand-building efforts. In this final chapter, we'll provide you with additional resources and suggest next steps to further your success in the digital landscape.

Additional Resources

As a social media entrepreneur, it's essential to continue learning and staying updated on industry trends. Here are some valuable resources to help you stay informed and enhance your skills:

1. Books

Explore books on social media marketing, entrepreneurship, and personal branding. Many authors and experts share their knowledge and experiences, offering valuable insights and strategies.

2. Blogs and Websites

Follow industry-leading blogs and websites that cover the latest trends, tips, and case studies in social media marketing and entrepreneurship. These resources can provide ongoing education and inspiration.

3. Online Courses and Workshops

Consider enrolling in online courses or workshops that focus on specific aspects of social media marketing and entrepreneurship. Platforms like Coursera, edX, and Udemy offer a wide range of courses.

4. Podcasts

Podcasts hosted by experts and influencers in the field can provide valuable insights, strategies, and success stories. Listen to podcasts during your commute or downtime.

5. Social Media Communities

Join social media groups and communities on platforms like Facebook, LinkedIn, and Reddit. Engaging with like-minded individuals can provide support, networking opportunities, and valuable advice.

6. Conferences and Events

Attend industry-specific conferences and events, whether in person or virtually. These gatherings offer opportunities for networking, learning from experts, and staying updated on the latest trends.

Next Steps

Your journey as a social media entrepreneur is an ongoing one. Here are some next steps to consider as you continue to build and grow your brand:

ADDITIONAL RESOURCES AND NEXT STEPS

1. Set New Goals

Review and update your brand's goals. Consider what you want to achieve in the short and long term, and create a plan to work toward those objectives.

2. Evaluate and Adapt

Regularly assess your brand's performance, audience engagement, and content strategy. Use the insights you gain to make necessary adjustments and improvements.

3. Explore New Platforms

Consider expanding your digital footprint by exploring new social media platforms or content formats. Keep an eye on emerging technologies and trends.

4. Collaborate and Network

Continue to collaborate with peers and experts in your niche. Building strong relationships can open doors to new opportunities and insights.

5. Give Back

Use your brand's success to make a positive impact. Launch charitable initiatives, support causes you're passionate about, and give back to your community.

6. Mentorship and Coaching

Consider seeking mentorship or coaching from experts or experienced entrepreneurs. Their guidance can help you navigate challenges and achieve your goals.

Your Ongoing Success

The world of social media entrepreneurship is filled with endless possibilities for growth, impact, and innovation. As you continue your journey, remember to stay true to your brand's identity, values, and mission. Your authenticity and passion will continue to be your most significant assets.

13

Summary

Chapter 1: Introduction
   - Introduces the concept of social media entrepreneurship.
   - Highlights the potential for individuals to build successful brands and businesses online.

Chapter 2: Defining Your Niche
   - Emphasizes the importance of choosing a niche that aligns with your passion, expertise, and values.
   - Offers tips on niche selection and validation.

Chapter 3: Creating Compelling Content
   - Explains the significance of high-quality, engaging content.
   - Provides strategies for content creation and the role of storytelling.

Chapter 4: Growing Your Audience
   - Highlights the importance of a strong and engaged audience.
   - Offers strategies for audience growth, including consistency, engagement, and collaborations.

Chapter 5: Monetizing Your Online Presence
   - Explores various monetization methods, such as sponsored content,

affiliate marketing, and selling products or services.

- Encourages diversifying income streams and maintaining transparency.

Chapter 6: Building a Strong Brand Identity

- Discusses the role of brand identity, including name, logo, values, tone, and mission.

- Stresses the importance of consistency and authenticity.

Chapter 7: Scaling Your Brand and Business

- Explains the significance of scaling for growth and impact.

- Offers strategies for scaling, including diversification, collaborations, and automation.

Chapter 8: Staying Relevant in the Digital Landscape

- Discusses the dynamic nature of the digital world and the need for continuous learning and adaptation.

- Provides strategies for staying relevant, cultivating resilience, and preparing for the future.

Chapter 9: Managing Challenges and Navigating Pitfalls

- Acknowledges common challenges faced by social media entrepreneurs, such as burnout, algorithm changes, and competition.

- Offers strategies for handling challenges and building resilience.

Chapter 10: Conclusion and Looking Ahead

- Celebrates achievements and emphasizes the ongoing nature of the journey.

- Provides a roadmap for ongoing success, including embracing change, cultivating resilience, and prioritizing quality.

Chapter 11: Additional Resources and Next Steps

- Offers additional resources for continuous learning and growth, including books, blogs, courses, and podcasts.

- Suggests next steps, such as setting new goals, exploring new platforms, and giving back to the community.

Chapter 12: Summary
- Summarizes the key takeaways and insights from each chapter.
- Encourages the reader to continue learning, adapting, and creating with authenticity and passion in the world of social media entrepreneurship.

www.ingramcontent.com/pod-product-compliance
Lightning Source LLC
LaVergne TN
LVHW010437070526
838199LV00066B/6059